Your Gifts

Are Not

Your Purpose

Workbook

Your Gifts Are Not Your Purpose Workbook

Laval W. Belle

ISBN: 978-0-692-92766-3

For speaking, seminars, and interviews
email wesleybelle@hotmail.com
website www.lavaldreams.com
8549 Wilshire Blvd., Suite 1442
Beverly Hills, CA 90211

Contents

Acknowledgements

I'd like to give my incomprehensible gratitude to God for His unwavering eternal love.

Thanks to my loving mother, who never left me or my siblings. I love you, Majean.

To my loving six children, thank you for a love I truly don't deserve.

To my editors, Erika Dowdell and Lisa Beasley, thank you for your invaluable work on this project.

Thank you to Bishop Charles E. Blake, who has been my pastor for almost thirty years. You are such a role model on and off the world stage.

Thank you to Dr. Judith McAllister for watering the seeds of my first presentation, *Your Gifts Are Not Your Purpose.*

To the countless senior citizens who fed me while growing up in St. Louis, MO.

Thank you, Ernest L. Thomas. You're like a big brother to me.

Thank you to all who purchased the first *Gift* book over the years. I am so encouraged by your support.

Finally, thank you to all my family and friends. The *Gift Workbook* is the fruit of all your love and encouragement. I love you all.

Introduction

After pursuing a music career as a drummer with all my heart, I discovered that my musical gift was *not* my purpose. I received this revelation while working with legendary vocalist Philip Bailey of Earth, Wind & Fire. As a result of that life-altering revelation in 1998, I felt compelled to share and write my first book entitled *Your Gifts Are Not Your Purpose*. That book was written almost twenty years ago. I've learned and experienced so much more since that time, and now I feel inspired to build on the topic of *Your Gifts Are Not Your Purpose* in a **workbook** format.

In the Preface of the first book, I wrote: "The rest is history and still unfolding." At the time, I did not know exactly what that meant. However, two decades later, it's now time to share the unfolding through the *Your Gifts Are Not Your Purpose Workbook,* and we can do it together.

We were all created for a particular reason. "Gifts" are what we are *created to do,* and "purpose" is what we are *created for*. There are three categories of gifts: natural gifts, talents, and spiritual gifts. Most people seldom discover or exercise gifts in all three categories. We spend so much time maximizing our natural gifts first because they come with natural instincts and abilities, and we don't have to work for them. Some people progress further and find that they possess many talents. And those of us who see the world through the eyes of God realize that we are created with spiritual gifts to advance the activities of our Creator.

We should all remember the words of wise King Solomon, *"A man's gift makes room for him."*[1] **Makes "room"** for what? I believe that metaphorically the "room" is *purpose*. Your gifts in each of the three categories facilitate your purpose.

Let's take a journey and clearly identify what your natural gift, talents, and spiritual gifts are. We will unleash the full arsenal of your talents and spiritual gifts, which will equip you for your created purpose.

1 Proverbs 18:16 (NKJV).

CHAPTER ONE

THE NATURAL GIFT

Every person is born with what I call a **natural gift**. It's not the gift of choice. It's the gift the Creator bestowed on you. No one taught you the abilities of your natural gift; you were born with them.

Think of it this way: You were born with the color of your hair, your particular way of thinking, your individualized walk, and your own unique smile. Your parents, family, and native land were none of your choosing. You were born into, and with, those qualities and circumstances. So, it is the same with your natural gift. Your natural gift has nothing to do with race, religion, culture, wealth, or social status.

Let's Define Gift. A gift is something that is given. It's a **natural endowment** or **talent**. The root word **"endow"** means to furnish or equip as with talents or natural gifts.[2]

The word "natural," as it relates to the gift, is interchangeable with talent. People often say to me, "Laval, you are really talented on the drums," or in the same breath, "Laval, you are really gifted." However,

2 The Oxford American Dictionary of Current English. Oxford University Press, Inc. 1999.

talents are distinct from natural gifts. (I will explain this in Chapter Two.)

The *Oxford American Dictionary* defines gift as "**a natural ability** or **talent.**"[3] "Gifted" is defined as "exceptionally talented or intelligent."[4]

A person may also naturally possess a number of gifts, or find that he or she is "gifted" in more than one area. But, there will always be one dominant talent or gift that stands above the rest, and that dominate gift is the natural gift.

The natural gift is the part of you that differentiates you from every other person. Your unique qualities are given at conception and are connected to your natural abilities and potential. Your gift, in essence, is who you are.

---

3 Frank R. Abate, ed. The Oxford American Dictionary of Current English, 3rd Edition (Connecticut: Oxford University Press, Inc., 1999).
4 Ibid.

Review

There Are Three Categories of Gifts

1. Natural Gifts
2. Talents
3. Spiritual Gifts

- The natural gift is the gift you were born with.
- You don't determine your natural gift; your natural gift determines you.
- The words "gift" and "talent" are interchangeable.
- We are born with both natural gifts and talents.
- The natural gift dominates all other birth-given talents.

What Is the Purpose of the Natural Gift?

Most of us readily accept the notion that each person is born for a particular purpose. However, not only were you created for a purpose, but your **gifts** were also.

The writer James puts it this way, *"Every good and every perfect gift is from Above, and comes down from the Father of lights, with whom there is no variation or shadow of turning."*[5]

5 James 1:17 (NKJV).

First, James lets us know that every gift is good or perfect (which includes all the talents) and comes from our **Creator.**

Second, James makes it clear that we don't determine our gifts. We don't have the option of changing our gifts. He says there is **no variation.** We can't go back to the Creator and exchange our gifts for the ones we want, like items in a department store.

Your natural gift has a way of navigating your life.

As King Solomon said, *"A man's gift makes room for him and brings him before great men."*[6]

Now, Solomon used the Hebrew word **"mattan,"** meaning a present; gift (to give, reward).[7]

I'd like to apply his principle metaphorically. Solomon communicates that **your gift** will make room for you. Let's take a closer look at this passage. Solomon is referring to a man's (male or female) gift, which is singular, meaning your own personal gift. It's possessive — not all the gifts, but a particular gift.

This kind of gift is not something a person stumbles upon; it's a gift that is clearly thought out. It's provided for a purpose, metaphorically or literally. Solomon goes on to say, "Your gift makes room for you." This is not

6 Proverbs 18:16 (NKJV).
7 James Strong, *Strong's Exhaustive Concordance of the Bible.* (Connecticut: Thomas Nelson, 1990).

anyone else, but you. So, if you apply your natural gift to this passage, your natural gift, talents, and qualities (not so much you) will make room for you.

This is why it is so important to understand the power and necessity of identifying the natural gift. The natural gift is personal. Remember, it's the gift or ability you were created to do. It's difficult to exercise an ability if you are unaware of its function or purpose.

So, the primary purpose of the natural gift is to make room for you. The natural gift is like your advertisement or **brand**. It draws attention to you. Your natural gift is a vehicle that provides opportunities designed for you. The opportunities themselves are tailor-made for you. Identifying the natural gift is crucial so that you can navigate your decision-making process to avoid unnecessary pitfalls.

The natural gift comes equipped with ability and limited skill. It's your responsibility to perfect your gift with study and practice. The musician David played skillfully and was faithful to his craft. "**Skill**" is defined as expertise; practiced ability; or facility in an action.[8]

It's important to practice and sharpen the natural gift so that when opportunities present themselves you are well

8 Frank R. Abate, ed. The Oxford American Dictionary of Current English, 3rd Edition (Connecticut: Oxford University Press, Inc., 1999).

prepared to seize the moment. Keep in mind it's your personal gift, unlike all other talents.

Example of Perfecting the Natural Gift – My Story

We all must perfect our natural gifts through discipline and determination. The more you put into perfecting your natural gift, the more doors will open and broaden your perspective.

Think about the awesome abilities and skill-sets you were created with. Think about how much stronger your gift becomes when your skill is used to its maximum potential. The Creator endowed you with this awesome self-contained gift, with infinite possibilities. How, when, and where you use it is up to you.

I was born with the natural gift of drumming. I never took a drum lesson. However, I practiced every day after school, from elementary school through high school. Fortunately, when I was a freshman in high school, the church I attended gave me a key to the building so that I could practice whenever I wanted. I spent hours practicing rudiments and exercises every day, and I became better and better. I perfected my craft, and as a result, playing the drums opened many doors for me.

I left St. Louis at the age of 19 to make a living and pursue a music career as a drummer. I lived, worked, and booked gigs in a number of cities before eventually settling in Miami, FL, where I played drums for the late Pastor David Epley (who was also my godfather) and his church. In Miami, I was exposed to authentic Caribbean and Central and South American music and rhythms that added new layers of proficiency to my craft.

Frustrated with regional work and seemingly no national or international exposure, I decided to move to Los Angeles.

There I had the opportunity to perform with some of the greatest artists in the music industry, such as Bette Midler, George Benson, Engelbert Humperdinck, Barry White, Chaka Khan, Aretha Franklin, Andre Crouch, Billy Preston, and Kirk Franklin, just to name a few. The natural gift of music afforded me the experience of traveling all over the world to numerous places, like Istanbul, South Africa, and Japan, with world-class musicians.

As a young man with very little financial means, I took advantage of a principle that is available to everyone: **Practice and determination lead to experience and exposure.**

Experience and exposure are some of the greatest life institutions we will ever attend. While traveling the globe, I saw how others lived and how they thought, and I was afforded the opportunity to share my gift of drumming with them. There was an exchange of ideas and culture that we only learn by leaving our own comfort zone. Most importantly, I learned how other artists expressed themselves through the arts and through drumming.

Just as it happened for me, your uniquely designed gift will make room for you as well, and even more so when it is perfected. No one can do what you do like you do it.

Review

The Purpose of the Natural Gift Is:

- To navigate your life
- To attract opportunities
- To make room for you
- To identify your created gift
- To perfect natural abilities
- What actions can you take to perfect your natural gift? _____

  _____

  _____

  _____

The Gift Formula

I have created a gift formula applicable to any person in the past, present, or future. We learned earlier in this chapter that our gifts and talents are divided into three categories: **natural gifts, talents** and **spiritual gifts**. Let's work through the formula together and use the great Earvin "Magic" Johnson as our subject as we focus on the natural gift.

What Is the Natural Gift of Earvin "Magic" Johnson?

1. **First, we will list up to ten of his strongest talents.** Magic is well known for being an athlete, entrepreneur, speaker, advocate, leader, actor, writer, coach and investor.

2. Now, let's focus and narrow things down a bit. We will now **list Magic's three strongest talents found in question number one.** I believe his strongest talents are: athlete, leader, entrepreneur.

So, What Is Magic Johnson's Natural Gift?

I can't say I know Magic Johnson personally, but I have crossed paths with him on many occasions over the past twenty-five years, and we attend the same Church— West Angeles Church of God in Christ.

On one occasion, while playing the drums with **Earth, Wind & Fire** in Monte Carlo, Magic Johnson came back stage along with Motown's creator, Berry Gordy. As soon as Magic saw me he said, "Oooh, I'm going to tell Bishop Blake." That made me feel so good because all the musicians, including the founder, the late Maurice White, asked: "You know Magic Johnson?"

On another occasion, we shared the same space at a local supper jazz club owned and named after well-known actress Marla Gibbs. I was a nobody in the music industry at that time. But I recall Magic's head almost touching the ceiling when he stood up. He shared that he had just signed some kind of extended contract with the Los Angeles Lakers. He clearly had a passion for business.

Magic explained in his autobiography entitled *Earvin "Magic" Johnson: My Life* that he used to clean offices for two rich African American businessmen in Lansing, Michigan. While working, Magic would sit in the big leather chairs and pretend like he was the boss. He never dreamed that some day he would play basketball for a living. His only goal was to be a rich business man.

Like you I'm sure, I assumed Magic Johnson's natural gift had to be his athletic ability.[9] But upon further investigation, I discovered the one driving gift and natural force that is a constant in Magic Johnson's life is **leadership**. As I write this book, Magic has just finished conducting a leadership session for the men at West Angeles Church.

---

9 Laval Belle. Your Gifts Are Not Your Purpose, 7.

Magic Johnson explained in his book, "I was the tallest kid in the class, a good athlete, and a decent student. The other kids looked up to me and I enjoyed being a leader."[10]

Magic went on to explain that shortly after being bussed to a predominantly White school, he quickly emerged as a leader among the Black students.

Because Magic's natural gift is **leadership**, everything about his experiences—his physical stature, his smile, and his personality—all facilitate his natural gift. He's a natural leader, born to win.

Can You Identify Your Natural Gift?

Everyone is created with gifts. For some, it's quite confusing when we have so many gifts competing for expression. I'm sure many wonder which gift they should focus on. The writer Paul instructs, *"God has given everyone a gift."* [11]

Let's Apply My Gift Formula to Assist in Determining Your Natural Gift.

1. List up to ten of your strongest talents that you can remember having since birth. (If less than ten, list as many as you can.)

---

10 Earvin "Magic" Johnson with William Novak. My Life. (New York: The Random House Publishing Group 1992), 18.
11 Romans 12:6

_____

_____

_____

2. Write down three of the strongest talents you listed in #1.

_____

_____

_____

3. Now choose the most dominant talent you listed in question #2. (Keep in mind the natural gift is a constant in every area of your life.)

   Here are some examples: music, creating, leading, making people laugh, writing, helping, giving, singing, teaching, speaking, modeling, advocating, cooking, athletic ability, chemistry, math, etc.

4. **So, What Is Your Natural Gift?**

_____

_____

_____

CONGRATULATIONS! You've just taken the first step in establishing your purpose, by discovering your natural gift.

Review

- The natural gift has nothing to do with race, religion, sex, wealth, status, etc.
- Every natural gift comes from the Creator.
- The gift formula will help you identify gifts in each of the three gift categories.
- Sometimes your natural gift will appear to be the same as your natural talent.
- What is Magic Johnson's natural gift?

_____

CHAPTER TWO

TALENTS

A talent is a gift of _investment_. Anything you put your time into developing (e.g., a talent) is an investment. Entrepreneurship, writing, and speaking are all talents I have acquired. I never had a desire to write anything growing up. But as an adult, I have written and published six books. I have also assisted others with completing books and telling their stories. My writing talent has afforded me great wealth and security. My natural gift is music, but my talents continue to bring me wealth.

Remember, our natural gift is connected to our brand and opportunities. A talent is a gift of choice, or a gift we acquire or learn. We pursue talents because they are fun, and they bring us pleasure. You can learn how to play the piano, sing, speak, or lead a nation. You can even teach yourself how to fly a plane! Yes, you really can! Most importantly, you can train yourself on how to **think successfully** by exercising your multiple talents.

Some people are born with talent and abilities. Still other talents are acquired and desired. For example, Magic Johnson, as you recall, has a strong propensity for business. I believe he was born with that talent. He was also a great athlete, clearly born with those abilities. Magic also acquired other talents, such as acting, being a talk show host, and writing, to name a few. However, these are not talents that Magic is necessarily known for.

It often happens that many great actors desire to sing, and many great singers try their hand at acting. So, our access to talents is endless, and the only qualification needed for those talents is simply **desire**.

I would like to highlight one distinct characteristic or difference between talents and the other gift categories.

In my first gift book, I have a chapter entitled **"Jesus, the Entrepreneur."**[12] The **master** taught his followers this great parable that I would like to share with you.

*"For the **kingdom of heaven** is like a man traveling to a far country, who called his own servants and delivered his goods to them. And to one he gave five talents, to another two, and to another one, each according to his own ability; and immediately he went on a journey."*[13]

Notice in this allegory that the master gave talents according to the servants' abilities. I'm convinced the same is true with our Creator. Talents are given to you and me based on our own ability. Let's observe four points here:

12 Laval Belle, Your Gifts Are Not Your Purpose (Los Angeles: Caring Ministries, 1998), 88.
13 Matthew 25:24-15 (NKJV).

1. The master and the servants functioned outside their **comfort zone**. You have to be willing to try something different somewhere else.

2. The master is quite familiar with all three servants. The Creator is well aware of the natural talents He's bestowed on you.

3. Talents are still the property of the master, which makes servants (you and me) stewards of those talents. ***Your talents are a down payment on your future.***

4. None of the servants had the same amount of talents or abilities. Don't justify how many talents you have based on the amount of talents others have.

You have to exercise and invest **all** your talents. The Master continues to share with his followers:

> *"Then he who had received the five talents went and traded with them, and made another five talents. And likewise he who had received two gained two more also. But he who had received one went and dug in the ground, and hid his lord's money.*
>
> *After a long time the lord of those servants came and settled accounts with them. So he who had received five talents came and brought five other talents, saying, 'Lord, you delivered to me*

five talents; look, I have gained five more talents besides them.'

*His lord said to him, 'Well done, good and faithful servant; you were faithful over a few things, **I will** make you ruler over many things. Enter into the joy of your Lord.'*

He also who had received two talents came and said, 'Lord, you delivered to me two talents; look, I have gained two more talents besides

them.' His lord said to him, 'Well done, good and faithful servant; you have been faithful over a few things. I will make you ruler over many things. Enter into the joy of your Lord.'"[14]

Talents Create Rulers and Wealth

Let's highlight the Master's lesson:

1. Talents were given for the purpose of **investments**. Likewise, your created talents are to be invested, and you are to exercise them and expect a return.

2. No matter how long it takes, the Master will return to inspect His investments. The Creator will require an accounting of your talents.

3. The Master rewarded the servants who were faithful. You will be rewarded for maximizing your talents.

---

14 Matthew 25:16-23 (NKJV).

4. The servants were awarded wealth and ownership as a result of their investments. Your talents will transform you from a **consumer** to an **investor**.

5. The servants experienced joy as a result of their faithfulness. Faithful stewardship of your talents will produce joy and financial stability.

Consequences of Inactive Talents

Inactive talents only produce fear, financial bondage, and sometimes devastating consequences.

> *"Then he who had received the one talent came and said, 'Lord, I knew you to be a hard man, reaping where you have not sown, gathering where you have not scattered seed. And I was **afraid**, and went and hid your talent in the ground. Look, there you have what is yours.'*
>
> *But his lord answered and said to him, 'You wicked and lazy servant, you knew that I reap where I have not sown, and gather where I have not scattered seed. So you ought to have deposited my money with the bankers, and at my coming I would have received back my own with interest.*
>
> *Therefore take the talent from him, and give it to him who has ten talents. 'For everyone who has, more will be given, and he will have abundance;*

but from him who does not have, even what he has will be taken away.'"[15]

Consequences Driven by Fear

1. The servant can't tell the lord what to do with even one talent—he was making excuses. Even if you feel your one talent is non-productive, maximize it anyway.

2. The servant was motivated by fear and did not invest his lord's resources. Fear, at its best, produces **death**. That's what the **ground** symbolizes in this parable.

3. The servant with one talent was characterized as lazy and wicked. It's an insult to your Creator when you fail to utilize your talents, only to take them to your grave with you.

4. The servant was instructed to invest his talent. You will give an account for all the talents entrusted to you.

5. Not only did the servant lose the only talent he possessed, but it was given to the servant with ten talents. The lesson here is, if you refuse to exercise your talent, you can forfeit its ability and reward altogether. Remember, at the very beginning of

15 Matthew 25:24-29 (NKJV).

this parable we are told "to each he gave talents according to **their own ability**." Ability refers to how much talent one can handle.

Review

- Talents are natural abilities we acquire, choose, or learn.
- Most importantly, talents are gifts of investment.
- Your access to talents is endless.
- Talents are strongly connected to your wealth.
- What are your strongest talents?

_____

_____

_____

CHAPTER THREE

SPIRITUAL GIFTS

What Is a Spiritual Gift?

"Spirit" is defined as an immaterial being; wind, by resemblance of breath; a supernatural being.[16]

The spiritual gift is not so much about its natural manifestation, but about the origin and forces of its unseen power. The spiritual gift operates in the spiritual realm. I believe spiritual gifts are the **most powerful** of the three gift categories.

Your spiritual gift is supernatural.

Purpose of the Spiritual Gift

Spiritual gifts are designed to advance the **activities** of God. Paul puts it this way:

"Now concerning spiritual gifts, brethren, I do not want you to be **ignorant.** Therefore, I make known to you that no one speaking by the spirit of God calls Jesus accursed, and no one can say that Jesus is Lord except by the Holy Spirit.

---

16 James Strong, Strong's Exhaustive Concordance of the Bible. (Thomas Nelson, 1990).

And there are diversities of activities, but it is the same God who works all in all."[17]

Paul wanted his readers then and now to understand the **source** and purpose of our spiritual gifts. Unfortunately, the Corinthians at the time of Paul's writings misunderstood the manner in which the Holy Spirit works through individuals. They abused the gifts, using them for their own motives, pleasures, and power. "The Corinthians, often confused of the power of the Spirit, viewed gifted-operations of the Spirit as a compulsive possession."[18]

Keep in mind that the spiritual gift operates in the supernatural realm. This gift is linked to the **Spirit of God**. There are also spirits and agendas of darkness that exist for evil purposes. The kingdom of darkness has talented agents who advance their agendas as well.

For example, when Moses went before Pharaoh to secure the release of the children of Israel, he exercised signs and wonders inspired by God. Moses was empowered by the Spirit of God to perform miracles to attract the attention of Pharaoh. Pharaoh, on the other hand, had magicians who were inspired by darkness to perform the same signs and wonders.

17 1 Corinthians 12: 1-6 (NKJV).
18 Jack Haywood. New Spirit-Filled Life Bible NKJV (Thomas Nelson Publishing, 2002).

"Then the Lord spoke to Moses and Aaron, saying, When Pharaoh speaks to you, saying, 'Show a miracle for yourselves,' then you shall say to Aaron,

'Take your rod and cast it before Pharaoh, and let it become a serpent.' So Moses and Aaron went in to Pharaoh and they did so, just as the Lord commanded. And Aaron cast down his rod before Pharaoh and before his servants, and it became a serpent.'

But Pharaoh also called the wise men and the sorcerers; so the magicians of Egypt, they also did in like manner with their enchantments. For every man threw down his rod, and they became serpents. But Aaron's rod swallowed up their rods."[19]

However, the kingdom of darkness has limited power.

"So the Lord said to Moses, 'Say to Aaron, 'Stretch out your rod, and strike the dust of the land, so that it may become lice throughout all the land of Egypt.' And they did so. For Aaron stretched out his hand with his rod and struck the dust of the earth, and it became lice on man and beast. All the dust of the land became lice throughout all the land of Egypt.

Now the Magicians so worked with their enchantments to bring forth lice, but they could

---

19 Exodus 7:8-12, (NKJV).

not. So there were lice on man and beast. Then the magicians said to Pharaoh, 'This is the finger of God.'" [20]

Even today, there are people and organizations who dedicate their lives and gifts to advancing the **kingdom of darkness**.

Examples include cults, human sacrifices, speaking to the dead, genocide, money laundering, drug cartels, etc.

Spiritual gifts and divine powers that accompany them were never created to be used to worship idols or manipulate, control, or deceive others. **Talented** individuals who knowingly work in these industries of darkness have mortgaged their souls, usually for **money**, **greed**, or **power**.

The enemy of your soul has negative plans for your spiritual gifts, and competes for them as well. To whom, for what, and where or how you dedicate your spiritual gifts are at your discretion.

Spiritual gifts are designed and dedicated for the service of God.

---

20 Exodus 8:16-19, (NKJV).

Examples of Spiritual Gifts:

Fashion Design - "So you shall speak to all who are gifted artisans, whom I have filled with the spirit of wisdom, that they may make Aaron's garments, to consecrate him, that he may minister to me as priest."[21]

Builders/Masons - "Then the Lord spoke to Moses, saying: 'See, I have called by name Bezalel the son of Uri, the son of Hur, of the tribe of Judah. And I have filled him with the Spirit of God, in wisdom, in understanding, in knowledge, and in all manner of workmanship, to design artistic works, to work in gold, in silver, in bronze, in cutting jewels for setting, in carving wood, and to work in all manner of workmanship.'"[22]

Music - "...but be filled with the Spirit, speaking to one another in psalms and hymns and spiritual songs ..."[23]

What Talent Have You Dedicated to the Service of God?

_____

21 Exodus 28:3 (NKJV).
22 Exodus 31:1-5 (NKJV).
23 Ephesians 5: 18-19 (NKJV).

Review

- Spiritual gifts operate in the supernatural realm.
- Spiritual gifts are designed to advance the activities of God.
- Spiritual gifts are empowered by good or evil.
- Spiritual gifts are the most powerful of the gift categories.

How to Determine Your Spiritual Gift

Like the natural gift or talents, some spiritual gifts are received at birth. Such was the case with the prophet Samuel, who later anointed David as king. Listen to the words of Samuel's mother Hannah:

> *"For this child I prayed, and the Lord has granted me my petition which I asked of Him. Therefore, I also have lent him to the Lord; as long as he lives he shall be lent to the Lord."*[24]

Samuel's spiritual gift was established and dedicated by his mother shortly after his birth, which he exercised all the days of his life. However, this is not the case for most people. Yet, you can identify your spiritual gift among your talents using the Gift Formula in Chapter 2. Let's

24 1 Samuel 1:27-28 (NKJV).

44

utilize the gift formula and determine what King David's spiritual gift was.

Question one of the Gift Formula instructs us to list all of David's talents: <u>musician, warrior, wisdom, orator, handsome, leader</u>.[25]

David's natural gift was **warrior**. We know this because David fought with animals, family, kings, friends, and fellow soldiers. He fought all the days of his life, even for his son Solomon at the time of his death. How can we determine David's spiritual gift?

There are usually two distinct criteria we should look for when determining spiritual gifts.

1. Spiritual gifts are dedicated to the activities of the Creator.

2. Spiritual gifts produce supernatural results when exercised.

Sometimes spiritual gifts are not manifested until there is a spiritual encounter.

The servants of King Saul presented him with a résumé of a seventeen-year-old musician named David and recommended him to conduct a spiritual cleansing for the king. David had a reputation as a gifted, young

---

25 1 Samuel 16:18 (NKJV).

musician, dedicated to the will of God. That covers our first criteria.

Not only was young David, at that time, nominated by King Saul's servants, but prior to that, David had also been nominated by God. Here's how it happened:

> *"Then Samuel took the horn of oil and anointed him in the midst of his brothers; and the **Spirit of the Lord** came upon David from that day forward. But the Spirit of the Lord departed from Saul, and a **distressing spirit** from the Lord troubled him. And Saul's servants said to him, 'Surely, a distressing spirit from God is troubling you. Let our master now command your servants, who are before you, to seek out a man who is a skillful player on the harp. And it shall be that he will play it with his hand when the distressing spirit from God is upon you, and you shall be well.'*
>
> *Then one of the servants answered and said, 'Look, I have seen a son of Jesse the Bethlehemite, who is skillful in playing, a mighty man of valor, a man of war, prudent in speech, and a handsome person; and the Lord is with him.'"*[26]

The power of God was clearly manifested in David after Samuel anointed him in the presence of his brothers. This verifies our ***second criteria.***

---

26 1 Samuel 16:13-18 (NKJV).

"And so it was, whenever the spirit of God was upon Saul, that **David would take a harp and play it** *with his hand. Then Saul would become refreshed and well, and the distressing spirit would depart from him."*[27]

David's spiritual gift was music, and when he played the harp, it produced powerful results.

What Is Your Spiritual Gift?

_____

If you don't know or you're still uncertain, you are not alone. Oftentimes, our spiritual gifts are not activated until, like David, we are **spirit-filled**.

Review

- Spiritual gifts are designed for the activities of God.
- Spiritual gifts produce powerful results when exercised.
- Spiritual gifts accompany the anointing.
- Spiritual gifts require dedication to God.

The spiritual gift is also the talent that we have no ability or desire to perform. The skills of the spiritual gift are divinely imparted. We are divinely instructed to create

27 1 Samuel 16: 23 (NKJV).

or lead in an area where we have no experience at all. The ability is supernaturally released when we are called to an assignment by the Creator.

How is this possible?

> The writer John said, *"The Spirit will teach in all things."*[28] When Saul was divinely called to advocate and build churches for the followers of Christ, he had no experience in building churches. In fact, he had a reputation for persecuting and killing the disciples of Christ. *"As for Saul, he made havoc of the church, entering every house, and dragging off men and women, committing them to prison."*[29]
>
> However, after encountering a Damascus Experience, Paul was divinely tapped to lead the very movement he killed and tortured people for and voraciously fought against.
>
> *"Then Saul, still breathing threats and murder against the disciples of the Lord, went to the high priest and asked letters from him to the synagogues of Damascus, so that if he found any who were of the Way, whether men or women, he might bring them bound to Jerusalem.*
>
> *As he journeyed he came near Damascus, and suddenly a light shone around him from*

28 John 14:26 (NKJV).
29 Acts 8:3 (NKJV).

heaven. Then he fell to the ground, and heard a voice saying to him, 'Saul, Saul, why are you persecuting Me?'

And he said, 'Who are You, Lord?'

Then the Lord said, 'I am Jesus, whom you are persecuting. It is hard for you to kick against the goads.'

So he, trembling and astonished, said, 'Lord, what do You want me to do?'

Then the Lord said to him, 'Arise and go into the city, and you will be told what you must do.'

And the men who journeyed with him stood speechless, hearing a voice but seeing no one."[30]

Paul was called, chosen, anointed, and appointed by God. The appointment was to advocate and create churches for his former enemies — the followers of Christ. Paul recognized the power and value of the spiritual gifts when he established a relationship with God and advanced the work of the church.

Take a look at what Paul said in his letters to potential followers of Christ. *"For I long to see you, that I may **impart** to you some spiritual gift, so that you may be **established**.*[31]

30 Acts 9:1-7 (NKJV).
31 Romans 1:11 (NKJV).

Personal Testimony

For those of you who already knew your spiritual gift and its purpose prior to reading this chapter, I suggest this to you: The spiritual gift harmonizes all the gifts, and it should be accompanied by supernatural power that produces results. When David played his stringed instrument before Saul, the distressing spirits left Saul. The power of David's spiritual gift was evident.

I would like to share my own personal testimony of the power of spiritual gifts. Many years ago, I struggled to rid myself of the addictive forces of the enemy. I went on a three-day fast, drinking only water. My objective was to get clarity, specifically about my gift of drumming and the destructive forces that were tormenting my mind and interrupting God's true intentions for my gifts and purpose. Because I spent so much time perfecting my craft in music, my drumming became more of an idol than a service. I clearly neglected my family, friends, and quality of life. During the fast, I experienced life-changing revelations through my submission to, and pursuit of, God's designed destiny for my life. As a result, at the end of my fast, I was infused with divine empowerment that truly realigned my focus and gift of drumming.

Prior to playing drums at any ministry service, I went down to the altar to pray. The supernatural effect of my music back then compared to now is unmistakable. Music is not my spiritual gift; teaching is. But the Creator's divine impartation has certainly harmonized all my gift categories, and they remain that way today.

Recently, a woman came up to me after Sunday morning service and said, "I could feel the **power** of God in your drum playing." That's a comment that I often hear no matter where I perform.

Signs and wonders should accompany your spiritual gift when exercised. If your spiritual gift does not produce supernatural results, I would encourage you to dedicate yourself and your services to God.

Spiritual gifts are classified as spiritual for one obvious reason: They are distributed by the Spirit of God for service. Depending on the divine task or tasks, it's possible to possess and exercise more than one spiritual gift at a time.

There is no definite magic formula or spiritual gift test that can identify which spiritual gift you possess. The best approach is to focus on serving the Creator. The answer to discovering your spiritual gift is to simply **ask God,** because spiritual gifts are provided by God's Spirit. The divine gifts are spiritual; the service is natural.

The Spirit of God harmonizes all the gifts. At this point in your life, all the gift categories should function in concert, led by the Spirit of God, to facilitate your purpose.

CHAPTER FOUR

WHAT IS YOUR PURPOSE?

"What is my Purpose? **Why am I here?**" Sooner or later life will corner you and deliver you face to face with this age-old question. That's one of the most important or fundamental questions you will ever ask yourself.

Purpose is defined as an object to be obtained; a thing intended or the intentions to act; resolution or determination. It is also the **reason for which something is done or made.**[32]

Let's examine the last definition. We will modify it just a bit. Instead of focusing on the reason for which a *thing* was made, we will focus on the reason for which *someone* was made.

"Then God said, 'Let us make man in Our image, according to Our likeness'"[33]

You were created with the same eternal DNA as God, and you were created for *one* reason. There is a part of God that only you can reflect. Think about it. Most actions you take, conscious or unconscious, are done

---

32 The Oxford American Dictionary of Current English. Oxford University Press, Inc. 1999.
33 Genesis 1:26 (NKJV).

for a reason. You eat because you are hungry; you work for employment, which brings money. You speak for expression or communication. There are certainly other factors involved, but the motives are usually for one purpose. We spend most of our life learning so we can maintain and enjoy a quality life.

Everything about your life guides you toward your purpose, including your gifts. But don't mistake your gifts for your purpose. In fact, I believe **"your gifts are not your purpose."** Instead, your gifts **facilitate** your purpose.

I discovered that my gifts were not my purpose while traveling and playing the drums for the renowned vocalist of Earth, Wind & Fire, Philip Bailey. One cold morning while taking a walk in Kobe, Japan, Philip suggested that we have a Bible study while out on the road. I told him that I thought it was a good idea. What he suggested next changed my life. He said, "I think you should lead the Bible study." I'd never led a Bible study before. Philip said, Just teach on what you know." What profound guidance. His very words made room for my purpose.

I went to my room and pulled out a piece of paper to create an outline on relationships. Relationships was a topic I knew a little about because I had so many bad ones. After writing, I lay down and fell asleep, and I heard these words in my head, **"Your Gifts Are Not**

Your Purpose." I could hear and see those six words clearly. I spoke the words out loud and wondered what they meant. Then I saw my entire life pass before me. Inspired and enlightened, I got up and turned over the paper that I had written on about relationships and wrote the words "your gifts are not your purpose." The rest is history and is still unfolding.

Today I believe your life will be changed because there is nothing more exciting than when time and purpose intersect.

Your purpose should fuel everything you say and do. It is a divine blueprint of your life's journey. Your decision making should absolutely reflect purpose. It's the reason that I found it necessary to write this gift workbook. Simultaneously, as I create this workbook for you, I am also constructing a publishing company called Noah's Ark Publishing Service. The same way God inspired the title of the gift books, He also inspired the name of the publishing service, as I was flying home from a book-signing concert in North Carolina.

The workbook you are reading now is the first publication represented by Noah's Ark Publishing Service. As you can see, God is still providing dreams and visions for purpose.

Your Gifts Are a Down Payment on Your Future

When purpose drives your life, you wake up every morning with passionate, profound, and inspiring revelation. Passion fuels purpose, and inspiration motivates it. This, for me, is an optimistic way of life. If this is not the dynamic of your life, welcome to discovering and exercising your dreams and purpose.

The Creator has bestowed gifts and talents upon you. If that's true — and it is — then the Creator also created you for one single purpose. David's gifts and talents were not his purpose either. And Magic Johnson's gifts and talents are not his purpose.

I highlight this point because many of us spend so much time on our gifts that we inadvertently make a god out of them. Your purpose is something that requires **divine intervention**. It's a life task that you simply can't do alone. There are other terms that are synonymous with purpose, such as destiny, mission, journey, creation, assignment, etc. I give many examples in my first gift book in **Chapter Five** entitled, "What Is Purpose?"

We all have experiences, but if our experiences are not fueled by purpose, they get us nowhere. Let me share this with you; my talents afforded me many experiences, but without purpose, my experiences were just a perpetual roller coaster of trial and error.

Review

- Purpose is destiny, mission, journey, or assignment.
- The gifts will facilitate purpose.
- Every experience leads to purpose.

Running from Your Purpose

Sometimes purpose isn't something that you want to do. All I ever wanted to do as far as I can remember is music. At age eleven, while living in St. Louis, there was an evangelist who came to our church from West Palm Beach, Florida, named C.S. Upthegrove. One night, during a revival service, he called my mom out and confirmed her undisclosed prayer for me at birth. She had prayed that I would become a preacher.

I thought they were both crazy. I had just started playing the drums in my church without any lessons. As time went on, I played music all over the world, but the words the evangelist shared with my mom became louder and louder, and the pull to speak became stronger and stronger. Drumming was all I knew until I finally stopped running from this overwhelming pull to speak. It was something I felt that I could not, and did not, want to do. I had absolutely no experience in public speaking.

Not to mention, after many years of living a rock-and-roll lifestyle, I felt I wasn't qualified for God's service.

When I began teaching and preaching, I was afraid that no one would listen to a drummer. I was terrified of reading the Bible in public, but my true fear was of being rejected by others. My reputation wasn't very good. I was embarrassed about my past, and I was my own worst enemy.

Then I read the writings of Jeremiah, *"Do not be afraid of their faces, For I am with you to deliver you," says the Lord.*[34]

God is aware of our past guilt and shame. Through that revelation, the Creator delivered me from people so that I could be used to deliver others.

I'm sure there are others who are like I once was, uncertain of their purpose. But we all have a purpose, no matter who we are or what we've done. Moses murdered a man and had a stuttering problem, yet he was still called to speak and advance the purpose of God.

> *"Then Moses said to the Lord, 'Oh my Lord, I am not eloquent, neither before nor since You have spoken to Your servant; but I am slow of speech and slow of tongue.' So the Lord said to him, 'Who has made man's mouth? Have not I, the Lord?*

---

34   Jeremiah 1:8 (NKJV).

*Now therefore, go, and I will be with your mouth
and teach you what you shall say.'"*[35]

Moses had no speaking experience, yet he was called by
his God to speak to the oppressive regime of Pharaoh.

I discovered that playing the drum set was like one of
my many talents leading to purpose. The drum set (each
instrument) represents our various talents. Playing the
drums is my natural gift. When I put the bass, cymbals,
tom toms, and snare drum together, the instruments
become a drum set for the purpose of playing music.
Likewise, when we exercise our gift categories, it leads
to our purpose.

Review

- Sometimes purpose is not what you want or feel qualified to do.
- The Creator will prepare you for your mission.

Your Gifts Are Not Your Purpose

Your gifts are the greatest natural indicator in determining
your purpose. We began a relationship with our gifts at
conception.

---

35 Exodus 4:10-12 (NKJV).

We established in Chapter One that your gifts will make room for you. In reality, all the gifts and talents work together in concert to provide space for your creative purpose. In the words of Magic Johnson, "Because of my skills as an athlete, every conceivable opportunity has been there."[36]

Nelson Mandela wrote in his autobiography *Long Walk to Freedom*, "I quickly realized that I had to make my way on the basis of my ability, not my heritage."[37] Like Magic Johnson, Nelson Mandela discovered on his long journey to freedom that his gift was not his purpose. But his gift would make room for his purpose.

What Was Nelson Mandela's Purpose?

Let's find out using the Gift Formula one last time.

1. His talents were: <u>speaking, warrior, leadership, writing, singing, teaching, history, advocating, law (counsel), philanthropy</u>

2. His strongest talents were: <u>speaking, warrior, leadership</u>

3. What was Mandela's natural gift?

---

36 Earvin "Magic" Johnson with William Novak. My Life. (New York: The Random House Publishing Group 1992), iv.
37 Nelson Mandela. Long Walk to Freedom. (New York: Flashpoint/ Roaring Book Press 2009), 33.

Here's what Mandela shares: "I was no more than five years old when I learned how to knock birds out of the sky with a sling shot. I learned to stick fight—and became adept at its various techniques, parrying blows, feinting in one direction and striking in another, breaking away from my opponent with quick footwork."[38] Of his teenage years, he writes: "I discovered the great African patriots who fought against western domination. My **imagination was fired** by the glory of these African warriors."[39] Mandela also took up boxing in college. He had a passion for fighting. *Nelson Mandela's natural gift was being a warrior.*

What Was Mandela's Spiritual Gift?

Mandela's spiritual gift can also be found among his talents listed in question one of the Gift Formula. As stated in chapter three, the spiritual gift is the talent designed and empowered for the Creator's service.

Nelson Mandela's life was spiritually impacted and transformed when his mother, Franny, became a Christian.

Nelson was not Mandela's birth name. It was given to him by his Christian school teacher. Nelson was greatly influenced by two leaders in the church, Reverend Matyolo and Jongintaba Dalindyebo. Mandela writes,

38 Ibid, 9.
39 Ibid, 23.

"Religion was a part of the fabric of life, and I attended church each Sunday along with the Regent and his wife. My later notions of leadership were profoundly influenced by observing the Regent in his Court. My destiny was to become a counselor for the Sabata (chief), and for that I had to be educated."[40]

Nelson's spiritual gift was **in law (counselor).** Although at that time in his life he felt that his spiritual gift as a lawyer was his purpose: "My destiny was to become a counselor to Sabata."[41]

So What Was Nelson Mandela's Purpose?

Sometimes you don't find purpose. Purpose finds you. Destiny, as Mandela puts it, can find you through unforeseen **circumstances.**

At age nine, Mandela's father, Gadla Henry Mphakanyiswa (a chief by blood and custom), died. As a result, Nelson's mother, Nosekeni Franny, relocated him to what Mandela describes as the great palace, Mqhekezweni, the provisional capital of Thembuland. She placed him in the hands of a Regent (chief) whose name was Jongintaba Dalindyebo. Jongintaba offered to become Nelson's guardian and provide him with the same advantages as his own children.

---

40 Ibid, 20.
41 Ibid, 31.

This Was the First Circumstance That Orchestrated Mandela's Purpose.

Justice, the Regent's son, and Mandela became the best of friends. While at home from his second year attending Fort Hare University, Mandela's foster parent summoned his son Justice and Mandela to inform them that he had arranged unions for them both.

The young men rejected the advice of marriage and decided to run away. The only place to run to was **Johannesburg**. This was the **second untimely circumstance** that would place Mandela on a direct collision course with his purpose.

Time and place and a series of events would place Mandela in position to help start the ANC (African National Congress) Youth League and later lead the ANC's Armed Wing, which Mandela launched with a group of friends in December 1961. The ANC is a political party that stood against racism to battle the oppressive government system called Apartheid.

Nelson Mandela's Purpose Was Advocacy.

In 1962, Mandela was arrested for defying the government. Facing the death penalty, he was eventually sentenced to life in prison. The media coverage of the trial brought world awareness of South Africa's unjust apartheid system.

Mandela became an advocate for the Liberation to free Black and mixed South Africans. In February 1990, Mandela was finally released. After 27 years in prison, Nelson Mandela ran for president and became the first Black African elected president of a freed South Africa.

Nelson's **natural gift** as a fighter opened many doors for him and sustained him through his journey. His invested **talents** helped facilitate the resources needed to accomplish his mission.

Mandela's **spiritual gift** fought the dark, evil forces of apartheid. The light of Mandela's spiritual gift (counsel) empowered him to meet the challenges that threatened his **mission**.

Review

- Circumstances are the greatest facilitator of purpose.
- Gifts/talents work in harmony to facilitate purpose.
- Sometimes you don't find purpose; purpose finds you.

Names Impact and Influence Purpose

Another clue that can help identify purpose are names. As I mentioned earlier, Nelson was not Mandela's birth name. His birth name was Rolihlaha. It was a name given to him by his father, which means "pulling the branch of a tree" or "troublemaker." Mandela was labeled a terrorist on his long walk to **purpose**.

Magic, of course, was not Magic Johnson's birth name; it was given to him at age fifteen by a sports writer named Fred Stabley. Magic **collided** with a circumstance that modified his name and later influenced his purpose.

Johnson had his heart set on attending Sexton, an all-Black high school, but he was bussed to Everrette High, an all-White high school. Here's how Earvin Johnson, Jr. puts it, "For the first few months, I was miserable at Everette, but being bussed to Everette turned out to be one of the best things that ever happened to me. It got me out of my own little world and taught me how to understand White people, how to communicate and deal with them."[42]

Names clearly impact our destiny. For some, names are divinely inspired. This was the case with Mary, a modest teenage girl who was divinely inspired to name her first son.

---

42 Earvin "Magic" Johnson with William Novak. My Life. (New York: The Random House Publishing Group 1992), 26.

> *"Then the angel said to her, 'Do not be afraid, Mary, for you have found favor with God. 'And behold, you will conceive in your womb and bring forth a Son, and shall call His name Jesus. He will be great, and will be called the Son of the Highest.'"*

I don't know any name more life-changing or impactful than the **name of Jesus**.

Jesus possessed and exercised all the gifts and talents.

But His gifts were not His purpose: The **Man** Jesus was created to die on the cross.

Are you willing to live and boldly exercise all your natural gifts, talents, and spiritual gifts? Are you willing to embrace your mission and breathe the air of purpose provided by the Creator?

What is your natural gift(s)?

_____

_____

_____

What are your talents?

_____

_____

What is your spiritual gift(s)?

_____

_____

_____

Clues of Purpose

- Gifts and talents are natural indicators of purpose.
- Names impact or influence destiny.
- Circumstances often navigate the mission.

I would like to give you one more example of how unforeseen circumstances can influence purpose for those of you who are still unsure about your purpose.

It's the story of Lisa Blunt Rochester, a woman I read about in the March 17, 2017, edition of *USA Today*.

In the interview, Rochester said she actually started as an intern in a congressional office back in 1989. She got a divorce after a 20-year marriage and then found love again. Lisa quit her job, sold her house, and moved to China for a while, where her new husband was working. Not long after they returned home to the States, her husband ruptured his achilles tendon, blood clots traveled to his heart and lungs, and he died (unexpectedly in 2014 at age fifty-two). Lisa said, "**It changed everything for me.** It made me question, **why am I here? What is my purpose?**"[43]

Sometimes purpose isn't discovered because **we never ask.** Circumstances are oftentimes incentives that prompt us to ask the age-old question, like Lisa Rochester did, "Why am I here?"

Lisa shared that one day she was on autopilot. She went to a supermarket and saw a dad and three kids in front of her. The father had to put back a bunch of grapes because they cost $9. At that moment, Lisa realized how blessed she was. She saw a lot of other hurting people, and many were not able to make ends meet or live up to their full potential and make positive contributions in their communities. In her words, "I just decided I'm going to run. Instead of sitting back and complaining, I'm going to step up."[44]

Purpose is a conscious **decision**. Purpose requires active participation on your journey to **destined greatness**. Lisa Rochester, age fifty-five, became the first woman and first African American elected to Congress in the State of Delaware. Circumstances and a title change have facilitated Lisa Rochester's **purpose**. Today Lisa is called Representative Lisa Blunt Rochester; she's the

43 USA Today, "Delaware Dem Relishes Breaking Barriers." March 17, 2017, 3A.
44 Ibid.

great granddaughter of a former slave, and is now a congresswoman of the United States.

Review

- Sometimes we simply have to ask, "What is my purpose?"
- Purpose is a conscious decision.

> *"And we know that all things work together for good to those who love God, to those who are the called according to His purpose."*[45]

You possess the same eternal genes as your Creator. You were created in the image of God.

What is your purpose?

---

45 Romans 8:28 (NKJV).

References

1. Abate, Frank R. ed. *The Oxford American Dictionary of Current English, 3rd Edition.* New York: Oxford University Press, Inc., 1999.

2. Belle, Laval. *Your Gifts Are Not Your Purpose.* Los Angeles: Caring Ministries, 1998.

3. Gilbert, Martin. *The Illustrated Atlas of Jewish Civilization: 4,000 Years of Jewish History.* New York: Macmillan, 1990.

4. Haywood, Jack W. *New Spirit-filled Life Bible, New King James Version.* Thomas Nelson, Inc. 2002.

5. Johnson, Ervin "Magic" with William Novak. *My Life.* New York: The Random House Publishing Group, 1992.

6. Mandela, Nelson. Long Walk to Freedom. New York: Flash Point/Roaring Book Press, 2009.

7. Strong, James. *Strong's Exhaustive Concordance of the Bible.* Thomas Nelson Publishing, Nashville, TN 1990.

8. *USA Today*, "Delaware Dem Relishes Breaking Barriers." March 17, 2017 Edition 3A.

Made in the USA
Middletown, DE
03 July 2022